THE QUICK

First published in 2018 by
The Dedalus Press
13 Moyclare Road
Baldoyle
Dublin D13 K1C2
Ireland

www.**dedaluspress**.com

ISBN 978 1 910251 45 4

Dedalus Press titles are represented in the UK by
Inpress Books, www.inpressbooks.co.uk,
and in North America by Syracuse University Press, Inc.,
www.syracuseuniversitypress.syr.edu.

Cover image by Denise Nestor
by kind permission of the artist
www.denisenestorillustration.com

The Dedalus Press receives financial assistance from
The Arts Council / An Chomhairle Ealaíon.

THE QUICK

JESSICA TRAYNOR

Jessica Traynor

DEDALUS PRESS

ACKNOWLEDGEMENTS

Poems in the collection have appeared in *Acumen, Agenda, Banshee, A Bittern Cry, The Bogman's Cannon, Copper Nickel, The Irish Times, One, The Penny Dreadful, Poetry Ireland Review, Prelude, Rochford Street Review, The Stinging Fly, The Stony Thursday Book,* and have been broadcast on *The Poetry Programme* on RTÉ Radio One and *Poetry File* on Lyric FM.

The sequence titled 'A Modest Proposal' was commissioned by The Salvage Press as part of an art book featuring Swift's original text alongside these poems, artwork by David O'Kane, typography by Jamie Murphy, and with an introduction by Andrew Carpenter.

Alphabetical thanks to Abigail, Anthony, Billie and Declan. And also to Jane Clarke, Eithne Hand, Catherine Phil MacCarthy, Rosamund Taylor and the much-missed Shirley McClure for giving the work shape. Thanks to Cal Doyle and Adam Wyeth for knocking it into better shape again, to Jamie Murphy for bringing great artists together at The Salvage Press, and to Dave Lordan for the craic and the chats. And finally, to Pat Boran, Mary O'Malley and Helen Mort for their faith in the work.

CONTENTS

To Abigail

"The dead are not abandoned ... What you think you're looking at on that long road to the past is actually beside you where you stand."
– John Berger

The Life

Halfway across the Hogarth Road
the life flew out of me,

pitched itself into the dusk.
What grip did I loosen, to let it go?

What shape was out there speaking for me,
picking up my stitches, finding my lost loves,

lying down soft beside them in the dark?
Watching it go was a gift

sudden as rain on a sweltering night
and when it came back – cool wanderer

pressing through my skin –
I knew I had been lessened,

that I was somehow more alone
than when I had been divisible.

Symmetry

You move the shed, electrics and all,
to one side of the garden, then back again.

We argue, relent. Hildegard of Bingen
had visions of perfect symmetry,

shapes and colours, galaxy-infinite.
You see that same potential here –

for each petal on each flower
to find its match across the lawn.

But there are obstacles:
the bloody shed,

cussedly singular,
preventing your moulding

of the natural into the ordered.
Hildegard would commiserate,

as do I – knowing
what this mania means –

you seeing shapes and colours
in the corners of your eyes,

fractured auras, night-terrors –
before long, another seizure.

Nothing to be done now
but watch from the kitchen

as you wander in a maze
with no centre.

Witches

I. Shadow-play

A child
        alone in my room

watching on the wall
        the dance

of trees
        long since cut down.

II. The Witches Manifest as a Fry of Eels

I grew up in a bed
                    of electric eels
        who'd twist in their skirts,
                            writhing to escape.
Sometimes static
                would sizzle
                            through their skin; and if
you caught   their eye
                you'd see   the spark
                                    that lived there.

Each married   a shadow
                always in search
of a body   and my eels
        cried crackling tears,
                their voltage soaring
until the time came
                they'd pin you
with a stare   pull you close

                    fry the heart
                        in your chest.

III. The Witch's Love Song to her Ex

You're a punch-bag, a suit stuffed with duck-down,
a helium balloon in a furnace, but still you trip about
forgetting your vitamins (a pint is not a meal!)

and between your pratfalls (lost jobs, unpaid loans)
there are those tar-pits we all tiptoe around,
the abandoned wives, the children no one mentions –

because tar sticks and we don't like the look of your shoes.
You're a laugh riot! An ice-cube on a stove!
An unattended chip-pan spitting your gold into our faces,

and oh how it burns our eyes, but we hide it
in the tiny pockets of silence that line our clothes,
that keep us afloat in dark water

when we drag you, yet again, towards the shore.
And though your warehouse is bare, we are out here waiting,
we fixers-of-men, to greet each areshole with a toothy kiss,

to pull the stones from your pockets,
to replace them with cups of tea that scald your balls
and to stop your mouth with slices of cake

as we wrap a hundred scarves around your neck
and wind and wind until you find you're choking –
and isn't it only what's best for you. And doesn't it serve you right.

IV. Scrying

In our old bathroom,
    the tall mirror balanced

on the sink, behind
    chrome taps.

One day I looked up
    as it fell in slow motion

and I stopped it
    with trembling arms,

shrieked as its weight
    pressed down,

until my father heard
    and came to save me

from the danger
    of my own small face.

V. The Witches Demonstrate How Best to Catch a Rabbit

Wait until the poachers have it gutted, spitted, sizzling,
until they're lulled by the patter of fat on the fire,
then creep out of the trees, careful that the moonlight

doesn't catch the bowie blade you've greased and whetted,
(the night may be cold: thermals are advisable)
then grab a poacher by his cock and bring the knife

up beneath it, threaten to hack it, root and branch,
so that he'll bleed out in the darkness, with no ear
to catch his frantic prayers. Then take your rabbit: run.

VI. The Want

My mother wrote a spell
   for what she wanted,

put it in a vase
   on a kitchen shelf

to wait there till
   her wish came true.

Wanting to know
   what a woman might need,

I climbed up to read it,
   but couldn't reach;

when I dream our home
   the vase is there still.

VII. Trash-Witch

A back garden in the smog days:
as evening settles yellow on torn-up carpets,
on lead pipes and broken dishes,

a trash-witch steps from the midden,
knits herself a body, lurches through the back door
to where a child sits cross-legged on the floor,

while her mother tugs the phone's flex.
The witch drags her broomstick legs,
and with horseshoe hands

and masonry nails she snatches the phone,
clamps it to the hole of her ear.
The wire that has been a hungry gut

for our secrets gives up all it knows.
The hag turns to the child, receiver in claws,
collapses into rubble and paint tins,

and the mother can't bridge the gap
before the child puts the phone to her ear;
hears silence hiss on the line.

May the jelly   in your eyes
be eaten   by eels.
May your guts   grow fins
and escape   out of your arse.
May the springs   of your bed
slice your back   like rusted knives.
May boils   fester your balls.
May sleep   desert you
may you not have   one second of ease
may the closing   of an eyelid
be a scalpel   to your retina
May your enemies   shit on your grave
until   it becomes
a blackened   monument.

This we wish on you with the power of our mothers
    our grandmothers   all our sainted aunts
(God help you) and with the unformed id
of our gestating daughters   whose vision
is nightmare   whose magic   is cellular
    whose name is splinter
                        shank
                            scrawl.

IX. The Witches are Angry

They have taken
my father's

writing hand,
and in the kitchen

my mother
gibbers spells

over the cooker.
My father drives me

into a night
where we talk about

his life now;
the river beside

the road so black
it reflects no light.

Will you be alright, I ask,
as my mother casts

her frantic hexes,
and in the car

the river pools
around our feet.

The Diving Bell

Of the men who worked the port,
the bravest were the divers;
those who sought pipes

submerged in stinking mud,
their breath catching
in the bell's humid dome

while their kit weighed them down –
helmet curving vision,
the stinking rubber of galoshes,

always the danger of a spark or leak.
As sweat broke on backs
that hefted pick and shovel

beneath creaking tonnes of water,
each man's demon whispered to him
that if he lost faith in the physics

of the aching, rust-worn bell,
it might cave in;
that the Liffey, like any river,

begrudging stolen land,
might claim him as sacrifice
for the insult of sewers, quay walls.

Coal Divers, George's Dock

When the boat comes in
the stern grinds
against the dock,

coal-lumps scuttle
between iron and granite,
ripple tarry water.

With each tide,
two hundred years
of coal dust sifts and falls.

Hunting scraps of coal,
children brave the water,
teeth and eyelids clenched

against ink and grit.
Look closer, among
dirt-slicked waves –

the gleam of an arm,
a slip of leg,
a neck's tender nape.

George's Automatic

Oh she was always
ahead of herself,
not talking down but talking up

to her betters, smug vole,
eyes like pebbles in her head,
what man would look twice?

And to think now her prize
is that streaky rasher of a man,
like a cold breeze across your midriff,

blind to her but oh the *writing*,
they say, the writing
is what keeps him,

and I remember that day in school
she sat snivelling over
her blotted cursive,

and I thought then,
*who gives a damn
about handwriting?*

But she's gripped by it,
they say it's like
a current running through her –

when the messages flow
he pores over them for hours,
in that drafty tower,

looking for meaning and petting her
for her cleverness. *Would you
wish it on your worst enemy?*

Firstborn

Our child grows no bigger
than a loaf of bread,

is covered in fur,
has not learned to speak.

She has green eyes,
walks so quietly

that all I hear
is the scraping of claws

when I turn and she runs.
But I have learned

that my changeling
wants to be caught

and scooped into
my arms. I have learned

what rough love lives
behind her fangs.

Emma and the Tape Recorder

Thirty shut-in years
bring Emma to a hospital;
her lungs fold like an origami bird.

I think back to the time
her mother took her from the Home,
that Christmas visit

where in her wheelchair
she howled and howled.
And I remember

the dream where I was locked
in a wind-blown office
with a tape recorder on a desk

that howled and howled
and switched itself on
each time I turned it off

and I woke up saying aloud,
Please Emma, please stop,
though we both knew

there was no stopping,
that the gale in her bones
would blow all her life,

her voice trapped
in the echo chamber
of her chest.

The Coffin-Maker's Children

First, purchase your lumber. Oak or poplar or another hardwood is best. For inlay, choose whalebone or ivory...

Dishcloth in hand,
my granny recalls
a trip to the Céide Fields:

peat-pickled relics,
shadow-villages
pushing up through bog

like secrets wanting to be told.
Her stories map
a route beyond the real –

but my granddad's lip
trembles, he whispers
over and over,

all the dead children,
all the little children ...
When I ask her why he cried,

she scrubs the sopping dishes
till her tea-towel
whimpers on the glaze.

... plaques in gold or silver plate can be mounted and etched with insignia ...

My granny sees a girl standing by the fence that splits her
   schoolyard in two. The girl is smiling at her.

She hears	the crackle of shoe on leaf
She sees	the girl's bare feet
She feels	the nun's blow

                          raising heat from her scalp
       in the cold air

*…now choose your coffin nails. The choices range from simple tacks to
   ornate silver-plated thumbscrews …*

While my grandfather waits for his beating,
Archbishop McQuaid arranges
his enemies' coffin nails on his desk.

He lines the nails, bright
and sharp and hopeful.
It will be years before he has enough

to pin each sinner down,
but he is a patient man,
inspects each one like a chess piece,

stands them so their blue-grey tips
face the ceiling. My grandfather,
fetched back from another escape,

can't see the nails, can only see
the cane in the next room
that will whip the badness out of him,

leave him numb until the urge to run creeps back.
My grandfather cries, or doesn't cry.
He can't see the invisible nails

and the force of his principal's blows
doesn't unfix them from their place.
So, they multiply –

become real enough to wound,
until one is driven
through my grandfather's palm.

… for handles, brass or silver-plate. For those who eschew all luxury,
a hempen rope will suffice …

My mother is dragged
by her auburn plait
along a school corridor –
the longer her hair grows,
the angrier the nun becomes.

The nun gathers
the slack in armfuls,
hissing vengeful novenas.
My mother's shoes
screech on marmoleum.

The classroom door slams shut;
       strands snagged in its hinges.

… finally, a lining to cushion your loved one's final rest. Calico,
hessian or silk is best.

When she is forced from school
to mind her brood of brothers,

the nuns take pity on my great-grandmother –
give her muslin to sew into shifts.

It is secret work, mysterious;
she can't picture the skin of a nun

underneath their crow robes,
but she thinks of her mother's body

warm against her
in the nights before she died.

Her father has other ideas –
steals the muslin to line

the cheap deal death-beds that lie
propped against the tenement wall.

It's better business for him;
shillings straight into the barman's hand;

but his daughter is shamed
by the tautness of the Mother Superior's face

when she tells the nun the cloth was stolen.
The nun writes something down

in a little book; dismisses the girl,
who for years, will imagine it as a curse –

a black mark on the family,
                    cell-deep.

In Bath Cathedral

O reader stay one moment with the dead –
our bones are mingling beneath your feet
and we are all alone.

Stay with us while our knuckles roll
amongst pence and relics, over curses
scratched on tin or silver to hex a neighbour

for a stolen blanket. All the company
we have now is Minerva's stone head
that never suffered joy or entropy,

her brow smooth while all around us
hot spring water picks holes in bones.
Stay through days of rotting joists,

through bombs that make the air sing
with flying glass. Stay, though the nave
is scattered with broken saints;

stay and hear and remember –
our echoes chime around the world.
They sound through the breath of others,

in unimagined deserts and cities,
in Damascus, in Aleppo, in Palmyra.
Stay and hold vigil. The dead are all the same.

The Artane Boys' Band

Da used to swing me over the turnstile,
to see the Dublin matches. I remember
the sight of my own legs, dangling.

I'd never see much of the game;
what's left is the smell of men,
their coats steaming rain and beer,

being hoisted by my ribs above
the crowd, the pitch spread out
green and vast, the distance of it.

And every half-time the band
playing on the field, their music rising
and falling with the seaweed stink

that rushed in from the bay.
There's the lads, Da would say,
and he'd wag his finger in a warning

that told me these matchstick boys
made music because they were outlaws,
each cymbal clash a cry of *mea culpa*,

and I imagined myself out there with them
in this rainy coliseum with my Da as Emperor
giving the thumbs down,

shaking his head for the loss of his son
to that criminal gang:
the bold boys of the Artane Band.

Lord Haw-Haw

No one has told him he's dead.
I wonder if it's a kindness
to let him wander in his ill-fitting skin.
Sometimes I smile at him in passing
before I remember it's the scar
grinning at me, not the man.

Like all the dead, he's losing his language
or perhaps just gaining another;
when he tries to make a joke
his words come out *silverfish, woodlouse,
earwig*; but the tone is still there,
the old coffin-sneer.

Some day I'll dig out a wireless,
play his last sermon at his grave
in Bohermore. I'll bring with me his noose,
a bucket of worms to lure him,
and when he appears among the trees
flapping like a felted-in sweater,

and starts to answer himself
word for word from grave to airwave,
I'll shove him through the hungry turf,
dance him right down to the devil,
where he can gossip in the sod
to his raddled heart's content.

Man with a Stone for a Tongue

The soil is riddled   with listeners
and the birds mimic   your voice.
The hare in the night   hears
your softest whisper   and the fish
that swallowed   your signet ring
knows my name   is scratched   on the band.

When they carried you in
they made sure   your throat was cut
but could we trust   death
to keep our love   a secret?
I whispered   some words in your ear
took my knife   sawed the tongue
from your mouth   kissed
a stone   to slide   between your teeth.

When time enough   has passed
to know   my death is near
I'll bring you back   your tongue
so you can babble   in the ground
about my lust   and what it drove us to
but when I tunnel   through to join you
maybe the sight of me   will silence you
the way it did   when you put
your tongue   to better use.

Cuck

It started with a headache;
over breakfast I searched my forehead
with my fingers, traced circles.

The day a sweat-pool, skin amphibious,
the lights in the men's toilets casting shadows
where none should be.

My eyes red-rimmed – *is this sickness?*
That night I felt the swelling,
but couldn't bring myself to raise my hands

to my head, kept them clamped to my crotch,
covers damp against my shins,
no air through the bedroom window.

A half-awake half-life of blood
stirring in my cock, the pressure building
inside fever dreams of you.

In the morning, in the mirror, a change.
They are growing from my skull,
fawn-like, pressing through my skin.

Little goat, I think, *little goat, little goat,*
as I walk through the crowds,
avoid my reflection,

and though they all pretend
they can't see my horns, I hear
their laughter ghosting me with every passing car.

The Heroes' Chorus

We rose before the sun and walked the fields with nets,
collecting birds. We took them from the nests
where they huddled, dew-wet, left their eggs to cool.
Their bagged heads kept them quiet.

We untangled kit, blasted shadows with halogen lamps,
reeled out acres of cable, gaffer taped it uselessly
to sopping grass, wheeled speakers over uneven ground
to shove among foliage and hedgerows.

The first call we played to the dawn was the Hakka,
its music much sweeter than what would follow.
We augmented with the Barritus as described by Tacitus –
a guttural murmur rising to a wail.

As the sky turned red our base notes remained true.
An anxious moment as Cú Chulainn's scream soared above
the baritone, and though the speakers popped,
the sound tech who had forgotten his ear plugs

wiped a trickle of blood from his neck. We paused
to see and hear the day we had made, and as sun
yellowed hillsides we watched livestock writhe
as if sound had stolen their breath, fall still.

Then, the final descant, the hero Culhwch's battle cry
that was said to abort the living foetus, or turn a woman sterile.
We fixed our headsets, braced ourselves. The sound at first
was a ripping of the fabric of the air,

but then the recording seemed to falter,
the heroes' screams wavered in the vacuum of the sky.
We checked our gauges, all of which insisted
the decibel level would deafen, but couldn't hear a thing.

I let my headset fall, stared at the fields of fallen sheep,
heard only the breeze, the scurry of leaves.
The nets of birds, dead from their ordeal,
we dumped into a ditch.

Nimrud

When recovering in hospital
the steroids mutated the radio's

talk of beheadings in Nimrud
to a dirge in your ear,

till the words you learned
as a child poured from you:

The Assyrian came down like a wolf on the fold ...
Byron's rhythms beating drums in your veins.

You were never one to remember a poem,
but in that ward it infected you –

we tried to laugh the possession away,
as the radio sang of black-clad men

blasting their marks on ruins,
pulling wings from the sphinx,

slashing its sightless eyes,
only to succeed in redacting themselves –

much as the words of the poem
fell away from you when we took you home.

A Modest Proposal

I. I Could Name a Country

and by naming, bring it into being –
a country not unlike ours.

Driving on a summer evening
you might see the froth of elderflower,

the shadows cast by chestnut trees
that beckon memories of youth,

or hear a voice in the distance
calling you home for dinner.

You might feel the heat in the earth
tingle up through your feet,

and with it the sense that if you move,
the evening will be lost.

But in this country that I name,
as you try to pin that feeling

to one memory or another,
you might notice the shadows' stillness –

and yes it is true that in my country
the sun never sets, but burns

on the horizon, tarnishing the evening
to old electro-plated silver.

If you were to go there with me,
we would stop the car among

those elderflower hedges,
and I would take your hand,

guide you to where you might hear
the long-lost music

of your mother's voice
calling you home across the fields.

II. A Census of Values

What is Good?

Mothers, innocent babes, parents, parish, agriculture, sheep, black cattle, swine, farmers, wives, cottagers, labourers, roasting pigs, a good lover of his country, persons of quality, so many good Protestants, gentlemen of fortune, wives, mares, cows, sows, swine's flesh, bacon, gloves for ladies, summer boots for fine gentlemen, Lord-mayor's feast, merry-meetings, weddings, christenings, mercy, honesty, industry, skill, native goods, carcass of a good fat child, learning to love our country.

What is Bad?

Beggars, rags, thieves, the pretender in Spain, the present deplorable state of the kingdom, professed thieves, wanting food and raiments, the present distresses of the kingdom, stealing, Roman Catholic countries, Lent, Popish infants, papists, playhouse, the gibbet, dying, rotting, cold, famine, filth, vermin, the number of papists, foreign luxury, pride, vanity, idleness, gaming in our women, voluntary abortion, women murdering their bastard children, selling our country and consciences for nothing.

III. Breaking Point

To avoid charges of sensationalism
we work now solely in euphemism –
train our workforce to ring-fence

all sources of fear,
we survey our neighbours, ask them:
what are you afraid of?

Tell us your dreams, the shapes
that unfold into terror;
a knot in your necklace

become a creeping sea-creature,
emerging from dark water,
indelibly real.

And of course each knock
on the door a stranger
with one child, then another,

who fall dead in front of you –
these children that look like your children,
but have no mouths to speak.

Sometimes the dream is a missing child,
or a child lost and come back,
changeling-like, to accuse.

We jot it all down,
seek patterns in these gathered fears,
formulate infographics in lime or cerise

instead of blunt realities; the child's
lost shoe, a pool of corpse-thronged water,
we offer bright columns of profit and loss.

And so we decorate ourselves with
'fate' and 'war' and 'tragedy' –
as we sweep our roads clean of litter

and bed down with our animals
for the solace we find
in our own familiar stink.

IV. Tender Butchery

As my feet cramp in the stirrups
I consider skin, its layers

and mysteries, I consider
my own sensation splitting

within me and whether
I can feel the tear.

I think about mementoes,
about what we can carry home

and what we can't.
The finest gloves ever made

were stitched from chicken skin –
so thin they would fold into

a walnut shell, so gauzy
that the wearer could feel

an eyelash light upon them.
I am that delicate now,

a membrane stretched
to encompass all the world.

If I could take this moment
I would fold it like those gloves,

lock it in a walnut shell
crush it, or swallow it whole.

The world has no business
wearing my skin.

V. On Blind Quay

in the early morning
you can watch the women line up.

Most are alone.
They don't talk much,

and if you wait long enough,
you'll see the ghost of a galley

slide against the quay wall,
where ropes are flung

by a silent crew.
They say the sailors are blind,

so they can't see their cargo,
and the women gather

like penitents,
their eyes grazing the ground.

The day I saw it
the ship had sailed

before the buses started running,
before a single seagull

loosed its lost-child cry
to the morning.

VI. A Proposed Housing Algorithm

For our purposes,
let us think of the country
as a small white box and, within it,

millions of smaller boxes,
each with a dot of red
like the blood spot in an egg.

These are the building blocks of life.
Here, in my world,
they are clean, defined.

It is my job to fill some boxes,
and empty others –
in many the dots have faded –

these are the elderly whose needs are few,
who use less space.
We group them into nuclei,

along with those less solvent,
for comfort, community, warmth.
Who will be alone now?

⬉

They have given me
a bright room to work in
and my schema is almost complete –

walls bare as an architect's model,
within them,
ruby beads of life.

I've almost puzzled it out,
but must admit that if the box
were to be opened,

flattened into some new pattern,
some beads would be lost
and others would have

no resting place at all.
The system would fracture into
another unsolved equation –

all symmetry lost in chaos,
but beautiful, still,
in the way of imperfect things.

VII. The Camp

People once came here on holidays.
Can you imagine?
The earth's navel on view

outside the window, grass pocked
with mud, and nothing for miles
but bad weather.

When asylum seekers came
someone wired the walls
with a hundred flat black eyes –

how bored they must have been,
these cameras, watching
the slow waltz of imprisonment,

the petty squabbles,
the shudder of a waking body
on a cold morning, the horizon lifting

like a cat's third eyelid
above the frozen ground,
the glare of a bare light bulb

casting tableaux behind families
hunched over scheduled dinners,
as tablets rattle in medication vials

and children squall until a door is slammed.
Who was the monster at the centre
of this maze?

VIII. Breeders Wanted

We have neglected the simple
arithmetic of years; delayed too long,

or wanted too much, until children
have grown rare. You may smile

at the notion of God's punishment,
but we are evolving ourselves

out of existence. We are growing
into aged infants, our worries catching

in the fine lines we conceal so well,
and to what end? A potential future:

one man to every four women,
a dwindling crowd of teenagers

hanging around the outskirts of the town
like the saplings we cut down,

bleaching into barren age,
and children born always

to the incubator, diminishing
to transparent zygotes

expelled early, pulsing their frail hearts,
the black dots of their eyes

sightless and accusing. *Is this what you want?*
You have a daughter, fourteen, strong.

The future diminishes every day,
but she has more of it than you or I.

Don't wait until it's too late.
Put her to breed.

IX. The Waiting Table

When all else fails, there is this:
a table set for dinner.

See how the sunlight
flares the mahogany to blazing red,

how it glimmers on china
that holds the memory

of a hundred bloody repasts.
How alien, how elegant the cutlery;

imagine the weight of the fork in your hand,
the bitter prongs you slide

across your tongue. If you could paint,
you might cast this scene

as a *memento mori;* the light blushing
the claret jug to clotted garnet,

the yellowed gleam of the silver,
the grapes in the bowl clouded with sweat,

and somewhere, amongst the piled fruit,
the cyan floss of rot.

But you will never need to paint this;
it comes to you whenever you are hungry,

the polite and comforting ritual
of slaughter. The universal need to eat.

In baroque shade, among the portraits,
the other diners murmur to each other,

and you know you and your fatted heart
will never be alone.

Calais

They came back, you know,
the children of Hamelin,
miles from where
they'd disappeared,

with the worn air of those
who'd walked too long,
whose limbs had knit to rope
from hunger and great distance.

At first, we caught glimpses –
a face at the crowd's edge,
a figure at the campfire standing
just beyond the reach of light,

dun rags in the ranks
of knock-off western sportswear.
And when we tried to catch them,
a strange thing happened –

the faces in the crowd
merged until the migrants
began to look just like the children –
wolf-like, hollowed,

their eyes all making
the same accusation.
When the camp went up in flames
we saw them clearly

standing grouped
among the burning tents,
their revenant gaze, their question:
Where is home?

Nocturne

I remember the poppy   the poppy
you still see everywhere   but there were none
in the war   only mud and tunnels
making cities   and men in them
digging in the dark   the sound of shells
screaming   in the earth.

*

They wanted me
to go back
see the graves
like little matchsticks.
How could I?

*

Sometimes in the night
I think of them   the lads
all waking in the dark
with no one to talk to them.

And if I was to go there,
I wouldn't know
what to say   and I couldn't
bear to leave them
                    when the night came.

The Writer's House

I'm there again, the basement room,
this catacomb disturbed
by passing ghosts.

His family peer from photos –
rows of faces bleached
like ossuary skulls.

I hear him and his wife above me,
and, though the stairs have vanished,
know they might at any minute

come tumbling through a cupboard door,
appear crouched in the cold hearth.
I hear their noises in the air.

Outside, if I were to look, I would see him,
hands black from the earth of a grave,
holding, root-side-up, a stripling tree.

Swarm

Search for them in the canopy,
among meadow grasses,

you won't spot them;
the thousands of bees

that unzip the air,
follow the day's weft,

that rip the silence like cloth,
tug the tiny hairs on skin

with their ghost music –
bees long dead, bees soon to die,

as the ladder of evolution
reaches its vanishing point.

They hide here
among birdsfoot trefoil,

purple vetch, self-heal,
among hemlock and nightshade

and they wait,
these phantom bees,

between the dusty pines
with those who have

nothing to fear;
the numberless dead.

Using My Tongue

I

I am five and learning
that words   can be weapons
      I use them
on the boy   next door
                (I adore him)

I watch his face change
      before he kicks me
with such force
                      between my legs
      that the skin

all over my body
                      tightens
and the world
                      burns white

afterwards
I have nowhere safe
            to lock the words away
and they snag

                      lemon-sour
on my tongue's edge

II

We feel sorry for Adam.
He dozes all day at his desk,
hair and face the colour of sleep.

His father's a famous killer
who keeps him awake at night.
We leave Adam alone.

Nobody tells the substitute.
In the corridor she says:
Bold boys use the girl's toilets.

We feel sorry for Adam.
But everyone laughs, because difference
lives under your bed

and grabs at your ankles;
laughter can scare it away.
I stay quiet, but the sound

has caught in Adam's ears,
and I must be standing too close
because he turns and his punch

steals my voice, leaves me retching
on the chalk-dust floor,
and when we're all back at our desks

heads on hands in quiet time,
my aching gut asks:
why is it a punishment to be a girl?

Poetry

This suite comes with an attitude.
Can you feel it? It is a heritage
attitude, available to guests
on an honour system.

It has many weathers
and came here with this colonial house;
rolled here on lumber
when natives burned the old town.

As you can imagine,
it may not be compatible
with modern attitudes,
but do enjoy its olde-time quirks.

If you wake to find it's hidden
your contraception, don't be alarmed –
just an in-house joke,
we carry extras at a small cost.

It may also manifest
as a flickering light bulb,
furniture moved in the dark,
or an ice-sweat in the middle of the night.

Sit back, relax and witness
these rare natural phenomena –
some day we may wake to find
the attitude has moved on

to other hunting grounds,
so enjoy it while you can
and hope, for our sake,
that it outlives you.

Photographing the Dead

His hair askew, your father
must have roved his eyes about the room
during the long exposure,

past the photographer,
towards the clock on the mantel,
the motion somehow hushing him.

Your mother would later think it
the cast of a lunatic.
Of course, she stayed rigid,

the halo of her movement
barely softening the slit
of her mouth,

her gaze glowering out of shot,
at the thought of tomorrow's
hard slog, or the worry

of arsenic in the wallpaper,
lead filings in the tea,
crinolines and open fires.

But you, at the centre
of the scene, your eyes seek
something further afield

and the sideways shrug of your neck
suggests a nonchalance.
Your outlines are so clear

it is as if you are sloughing off
your dull-eyed parents
and entering the real.

I almost pity them, left behind:
all those years to fill with toothaches
and stillbirths, boils and cholera –

all that life shining
through their pasty faces,
and what are they to do with it?

Citizens' Assembly

We called a meeting with the Catholic dead
          got little sense from them
but it had to be done.

One woman in mob-cap and woolen shawl
ranted about Peelers   the price of flour
      a bewigged man condemned
the whoredom   that had left him poxed.

A fat man took an apoplexy over women's rights
        died all over again
while wan adolescents thronged the back
       coughing blood.

A lechery of priests were first to comment
McQuaid in scarlet   stepped forward
      to speak for us all   owned
they could not agree on anything   *except*

that no decision should be made without
the input   of the faithful departed:
life is too serious a business   for those
        with eyes clouded
    by a future.

Matches for Rosa

'I want to give it to Rosa Luxemburg, who loved birds and flames.'
— John Berger

This matchbox is a gift for Rosa —
I'm sending her a text first, so she will expect it
where she lives now, in a room
on the other side of water.

Even the dead can light a fire with the right tinder,
like these matryoshka matchboxes —
each one hiding a smaller lacquered case,
and a painted Russian songbird.

Perhaps each bird with its sloe-deep eyes,
its harlequin flashes of scarlet or gold
will be reborn as a phoenix in that other place;
perhaps, where the dead live, sparks catch quicker,

and, maybe in return for my gift,
this woman so in love with fire and flight
will send her blazing birds to my pyre.

Perseids

On Camden Quay,
a mother and her son stare
into the night.

I join them, look out over the Lee
at the milk-swollen moon,
seek meteors among

the clouds that catch
the city's excess glow.
The one flicker I see – a plane,

but the boy's face is still upturned,
and though the light
from whatever star he saw

has vanished in clouds,
or perhaps from the universe
long before he set eyes on it,

he grips his mother's hand,
his star caught
in the dark of his pupil.

Snow Ghost

Went downstairs
while everyone slept
to find the snow ghost in the hall.

How piteous his eyes,
their filaments dulled
by smog and soot.

His legs were wrapped in plastic bags,
every frosted incline
sent him sprawling.

O pity the beast, he said,
and then –
a penny for the wren –

offering me
the thing clenched
in his frostbitten fingers –

its starveling feathers
crisped by frost,
its shattered beak.

It's my heart, he said,
and yes I saw it was.
How we wept

in the half-light
for the death
of one small bird.

The Quick

The seed swelling in the womb
      the earth has made it
          the drift of lime into the pit
ashes soft on rictus grins

the first to speak   to taste iron
      on the tongue   to run
and the living   the bacterial living
      their stain   their voices

the dead   those dead and not dead
      walking the knife bridge
those who clung to the heat of the herd
      held their children's hands
          stepped   into silence

the cut   at the heart of you
      that tore with your umbilicus
the half-moon in your fingernail
      the sickle of your DNA

your blood's starfish sprawl
      and the heart of you   plum-heavy
built to stagger on

NOTES

'George's Automatic' (p. 25): Refers to George Hyde-Lees, W.B. Yeats' wife, and her automatic writing.

'The Coffin-Maker's Children' (p. 29): Archbishop John Charles McQuaid (Primate of Ireland 1940-1972) was influential in the drafting of the Irish constitution and has become emblematic of a time when the Catholic Church exerted much influence over the Irish State. Before becoming Archbishop he was headmaster of Blackrock College.

The Céide Fields in Co. Mayo are the world's most extensive Stone Age monument.

'In Bath Cathedral' (p. 33): *O reader stay one moment with a dead* is an inscription from a grave stone set into the floor of the nave.

'The Artane Boys' Band' (p. 34): St. Joseph's industrial/ reformatory school for boys was run by the Christian Brothers from 1870-1969. The Artane Band, made up of boys from the school, often played at Gaelic Athletic Association matches. Numerous complaints of physical and sexual abuse have been made by survivors who attended the school, and 'being sent to Artane' was a threat used to frighten misbehaving children.

'Lord Haw-Haw' (p. 35): AKA William Joyce, an Irishman who broadcast Nazi propaganda to Britain during WWII.

'The Man With a Stone for a Tongue' (p. 36): A Roman-British skeleton discovered in Northamptonshire was found to have had his tongue cut out and replaced with a stone.

'Cuck' (p. 37): A shortened form of the word 'cuckold', originally referring to a man whose wife was unfaithful. Currently used as an abusive term for men with progressive views, especially online.

'A Modest Proposal' (p. 41): A series of poems commissioned for the 350th anniversary of Swift's birth by The Salvage Press, and written in response to the provocation, 'What might Swift write about now?' 'A Census of Values' is a found poem taken from the words italicised in the original printing.

'Photographing the Dead' (p. 65): In the Victorian tradition of photographing dead relatives with their living family members, the image of the deceased was often the sharpest, as they didn't move during the long exposure.

'Citizen's Assembly' (p. 67): In 2017, a Citizen's Assembly was called in Ireland to establish whether there should be a referendum to repeal the 8th Amendment to the Constitution, an amendment equating the life of a child with that of its mother.

CPSIA information can be obtained
at www.ICGtesting.com
Printed in the USA
FSHW02n2229270918
52372FS